AMERICAN GALACTIC

AMERICAN GALACTIC

a poetry collection by

LAURA MADELINE WISEMAN

American Galactic
by Laura Madeline Wiseman

First edition, May 2014. ISBN 978-0-615-97036-3.

Cover by Christopher Coffey. Book design by Julian Darius.

Published by Martian Lit. For more information about this or other titles, visit martianlit.com.

Contents

Lots of people around here have been taken for rides in UFOs.

Charles Simic

Between Lands

It is the opinion of all the modern philosophers and
mathematicians, that the planets are habitable worlds.
Benjamin Franklin

I.

The Martians are mid-space,
afloat in the gravitational force

of solar orbit, a pull toward
planets, moons, belts, asteroids.

The Martians wonder where
to find purchase, where

their feet will dig into sand.

II.

The Martians wander from the Red Planet.
Some drive silver spaceships to explore
their moons.
        First they visit Phobos,
whose crater-scarred, rough body
moves West to East every eight hours.

In her Stickney Crater they plant
flags and snap pictures of her insides.

The crater spans six miles,
and is one half of its grooved faced,

the only face it shows daily
as it inches closer to Mars.

On the pock-marked celestial globe
of their second moon, tiny Deimos,

the Martians pound prints in the dust.
This terror moves every thirty hours.

Some Martians watch their friends escape
velocity for their closest neighbor,

a blue-green swirl that could sustain life.
Martians touch down in likely spots,

but the Red Planet waits. Canals dry up.
Their sides cave. Each summer,

polar caps recede. During the 687 days
of the year, Martian bacteria burrow

underground, seas vaporize and leave
behind enormous depressions that appear

as if nothing could live, except Martians.

I

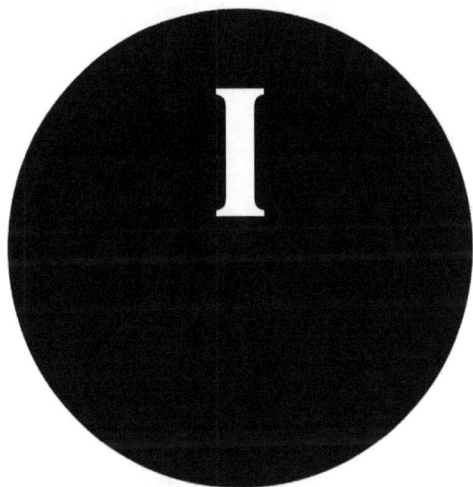

Long before the Martian invasion...
H. G. Wells, 1898

Warning

She might as well be on Mars.
John Berryman

Not ice storms. Not thunderstorms.
Not monsoons, tornadoes, or snowstorms.
Solar storms, they don't bother me.

Maybe it's because the radio says *buy*
water in jugs or cans of baked beans
and THIS IS A WARNING FROM YOUR...

Sirens circle every fifteen minutes
but nothing ever touches down.
The TV's red banner announces: no work,
no school, the city has surrendered

to the chaos of snowflakes and ice.
River water climbs into fields, roads,
a university. All of us swallowed by rain.

Maybe I should shudder or sob
or carry cyanide in a hollow tooth
or get in the car real quick and drive

for that one thing I'm going to need
when the electric lines loop through the yard
and drape over the neighbor's swing-set.

Even now I watch the trees gutter
and the wind tongues the house.
I can almost hear the words, something like:
The Martians have landed. You're free.

Rocket Summer: A Memory

He came in a metal thing that glittered in the sun.
Ray Bradbury

That summer I worked as a Girl Scout camp counselor.
I chose my name, *Mars*. White letters emblazoned
on a blue tee-shirt of stars, comets, and nine planets.

Week one, a black centipede twisted in my sneaker.
Week two, a bumblebee curled under my cot.
Week three, NASA arrived to train us to teach girls
about the rover and craters on the moon.

Week four, a howl rose up from the creek cavern
in the middle of the night. I wanted to follow it
down the ravine, to clutch damp limbs, to step
barefoot into darkness, to stare inside the unknown.

I didn't know what made the cries. A bird screech?
A preteen nearly murdered? The galactic ghoul?
A Martian spaceship killing a chosen few?

I could hear the calls from inside my sleeping bag.
I shook, hyperventilated, dreaming in the cacophony—
purple and yellow orbs flew, debris ricocheted,
asteroid belts spun all night—all that
                              until I came to,
the morning red and hot. I was still Mars.

Getting Out of Here

I always thought it would be in my professional lifetime.
Now I just hope it will be in my lifetime.
Gene Giacomelli, PhD

Scientists report early Australians
    burned flora to facilitate travel.
This shifted weather patterns

and transformed their continent.
    Their coasts remained lush green,
but their center became desert.

Maybe we're all really early Aussies wishing
    for far-reaching travel—electric cars, solar
power, and more ways to reduce, recycle,

and reuse. What's true? Does anyone enjoy
    the news: the ozone gapes, ice caps
melt, and storms recreate the coasts.

I, too, am America. I welcome
    its hummingbirds, snakes, sand dunes,
the Rialto River, and daily heat at 115°.

I worship the sun in moderation. I freckle
    coated in SPF 45, under a large hat,
and long-sleeved shirt and trousers.

And now I learn, that down the street,
    NASA plants lettuce in a lunar greenhouse
to practice gardening in outer-space.

After Watching a Martian Marathon on Cable

I don't know what Martians eat. They might eat
potatoes or human caviar. I don't know

what they wear to dances or how they move
their limbs in gravity or if beats propel them

to sway, gyrate, and touch. I don't know
what I'd do if Martians arrived at my door

or melted through the walls or crawled inside
me, turning me into them. If they called,

I'd probably not answer because of the number,
thinking it was that automated voice

to tell me, again, my warrantee is about to expire,
when I know my 1991 car doesn't even start.

Are Area 51 and Roswell big lies? I don't know.
Is Devils Tower? Do boys on bicycles fly

with one in a crate? I don't know
if Martians abduct us to cut into our inner worlds.

The Tabloids

Near Mount Rainer they move like saucers skipping on water.
Kenneth Arnold

They move in crowds and cluster together
in public spaces—the neon glow of strips,
the strobe of clubs, the dank of toilets.

When they talk their faces stay flat,
mouths opening as if they would speak.
Their heads are several sizes too big

for their bodies, slim arms and legs,
boyish in their gangly stride. Their eyes
never blink. If you can get one alone

you won't hear the pant of breathing,
no hot caresses, only that saucer stare,
part in this room, part adrift in space.

Their skeletal selves fill flashy covers
and exclusives in the check-out aisle,
an offer to gawk, to guffaw, to claim

you knew one once. All of us alien
in our fetish with Martians, the red planet,
beams of light propelling our eyes up.

Reality TV: The Trouble with Martians is they Don't Fit In

On the playground, they're the ones in the sandbox
full of cat turds. In the office, no birthday cards

decorate their cubicles, and at lunch, they sit alone
by the microwave. At parties, they're not spaced-out

wallflowers. They're the cluster of green bodies
gyrating ahead or behind the beat. They're in line

for the cash bar and clasp half-drunk domestics.
They're the few who sidle up and make small talk

with the neurotic seventh grade school teacher
or the nurse who covers the nightshift at the ER.

Problem is, wherever they congregate, humans disperse
like cockroaches caught in five AM kitchen light.

Creed: The Mission

Accept the limits of the landscape.
Grow moonflowers. Transplant rain
lilies. Always befriend stargazers.
Listen when the Big Ear speaks.

Think. Read with a roving hunger.
Never jump from a spacecraft.
Avoid deep-sea diving. Remember
Pluto will always be a planet.

Seed. Water. Compost. Repeat.
Shave only as often as you have to.
Build flying saucers. Take naps. Live
debt free. Wear comfortable shoes.

Believe in versions of the truth.
Breathe. Hold hands. Hug. Recycle.
Hope that if there are Martians,
they wouldn't be interested in you.

Arrival

*I mean, think about it: don't you want to believe that there's
more going on here than what meets our beady little eyes?*
Eleanor Lerman

When they arrive, it won't be at my house.
I'll hear it on the TV on a 24-hour loop
that replays the landing: metal ships,
slick and black with unworldly cargo.

For days the news hosts re-spin the event
with a history special on Martians,
eyewitness accounts, and embedded journalist
at the frontline. On the local college radio,
a low band story will cover police brutality,

how men in blue with face masks, batons,
and rubber bullets stopped the mob,
the men with pitchforks, how they freed
babies trapped on roofs due to the landing.

The pert blonde on the morning show
will look earnestly into the camera
and tell me she knows what I can do
in the face of an invasion on my street.

Then there will be a commercial,
two more guests, another commercial,

and then she says, fill your bathtub
with water, avoid your cell phone,

don't open the door to strangers,
and whatever you do, stay tuned
for more tips to save your life.

First Contact

These creatures are living Martians.
Octavia E. Butler

When the first Martians knock, I open the door
with a bowl of chocolate, suckers, and quarters.

These Martians are typical Martians: green skin,
long, thin limbs, and maybe three-feet-tall.

The Martian eyes glitter. I ask, *Who are you?*
The Martians stay mute. Then a Fairy, Superman,

and two Military Specialists crowd the porch
holding plastic gourds. I extend the bowl of candy.

Thank you! says the Fairy whose wings shiver.
She dashes down the steps into the night.

Then Superman, the military, they all leave,
but the Martians remain. I ask, *Where's your mom?*

I scan the street and note my neighbors
on their lawn pretending to be stuffed dummies.

As the Fairy climbs their driveway, they growl.
I study the Martians, glance up and down the street.

I do what any normal type person might do.
I take the limp hands and pull the Martians inside.

Stranger Still

The Martian gives me
    a heart,
a silver love

engorged with twilight.
    With two hands
in metallic gloves

the Martian offers
    this shimmering lust
to me, conceived

on an island,
    hard, small,
as wide as a dime.

The Martian says nothing,
    never asks
for a promise.

The Martian folds
    the heart in my hand,
then enters my bedroom.

Housekeeping with Martians

To keep the house. To domestic tasks listed to-do.
To keep working. To whistle and even sing.

To wash and dry the dishes by hand. To the shine
of wiped counters. To elbow grease.

To keeping chocolate bars in the freezer. To keeping
the peace. To making peace.

To deep cleaning. To light cleaning. To spring
cleaning. To clean pieces of paper.

To fresh litter in the box. To kibble in the dish.
To the lap of rough, pink tongues.

To the washing machine's whirl. To the heat
of fresh sheets. To coming clean.

To rearranging the furniture. To playing house.
To horseplay. To find yourself on your knees

catching dust bunnies that hop from reach.
To keep some for tomorrow. To keep all

the secrets. To keeping your word. To baking soda,
vinegar, and bleach. To vacuum patterns

on the carpets. To floors that glitter with sun.
To kitchen rugs shook to the breeze.

To clean hands. To more green hands to clean. To keep
a diary. To keep the house clean.

South of the Train Tracks

He is the spirit of the right Martian breed.
Ben Jonson

We've been learning how to own a home,
unlearning what we were taught before. Begin
with signing the mortgage for a split-level house
in a blue collar neighborhood—locksmiths,

electricians, fast-food cashiers, janitors—
all the necessary workers who keep a city
clean, fed, lit with blue light, and open
to whomever might need to get inside.

The job of a new homeowner is to repair,
undo, and upgrade. The original furnace
is the first to go. The stained carpet and pad
pull up easily. The fresh paint smoothes

the walls. Yes, we must call someone
to spray for roaches. Yes, we must save
each month to replace the roof. Yes,
the nearby power lines and factories

give us pause. But the welcome mat
and new bed of roses—all that we do—
lets the family next door know we're here
to stay and we're one of them.

A Star

Step by step, in Martian clothing, the two figures move forward,
pursuing their race against time….

I can never tell who he is.
For half a decade I was sure
he was Mork from Ork who drove
an egg-shaped spacecraft.

But then, he was a man
dressed up like a housekeeper
who spoke with a warbled tone
on his/her own puppet show.

Once he was a poetry teacher
in a private school for boys.

I will never forget him as a shrink.
In a bear-hug he said, *It's not*
you're fault. It's not your fault. I cried.

There was the time he taught
drag queens to dance at his cabaret.
And just last week he was a robot
who begged congress to let him be a man.

He's spoken in many voices—a soldier
who announced, *Good Morning, Vietnam,*
and a large purple genie—but never his own.

I know he's only an actor
assigned the roles he's been cast
in a script he didn't write, but I think
he's the only honest one

among us. Whether clad
in white lab coat or green tights
he seems to be saying, *Everyday*
I try to figure out who I am.

What Martians Wish

Maybe that they can settle here
in a suburban neighborhood—
everyone gets a PC, a green lawn,
a veggie patch out back to tend.
That the mailman will wave,
the grocer will fill their tote bags.
Maybe that when they line up
at the elementary in November
their vote will be counted.
That the sun shines bright.
That the nights are full
of crickets, owls, and silence.
Maybe that beside the bed
is always a stack of books,
a lighted footpath to enter
other towns, other galaxies.

The Martians Order

We shall not cease from exploration...
T. S. Elliot

new shoes. Six pairs
    of sandals, scuba flippers,
trainers, and heels
    arrive with padded soles.
Their three-toed feet
    slip inside to test
the hallway catwalk.
    Galoshes appear
in another box,
    rubber knee-highs
that suction
    to the linoleum.
The Martians cavort,
    and dash into the rain
to puddle jump
    slugs and night crawlers
aligned on the sidewalk
    like trails of falling stars.

II

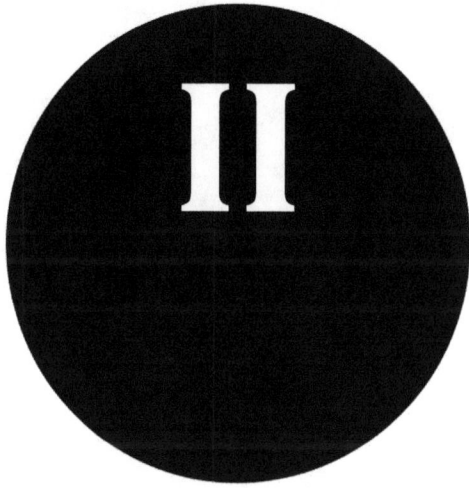

Here alien deserts slumbered.
Ray Bradbury, 1962

Why Not to Buy Martians Sundaes Topped with Cherries

They don't crunch or chew.
The smooth green skin

of their jaw stays still.
No quake of tongue

to whisk a wad from gum
and cheek. No dance of lips

on knife tip or fork tines.
They don't slip two stems

in the mouth. Their eyes shut
as their tongue swirls.

No flip. No spin. No hand
to pluck the wet knot

from tongue's end. No cocked
brow. No grin spreads

to lure and tempt a thought,
to coax a slow walk home

when hands might touch.
They could, but they won't.

Protest

How'd the moon get there? How'd the sun get there? How'd it get
there? Can you explain it to me? How come we have that and
Mars doesn't have it?
Bill O'Reilly

There's a movement
to slay the Martians.

City folks gather
on the capitol steps

wielding pitchforks.
These Martians

aren't human beings,
a woman claims.

Her child grabs
at the microphone

as she hiccups.
The pro-Martian group pickets

on the opposing corner.
They clutch homemade signs

stapled to paint sticks.
Among them, are Martians

disguised as humans
in Ronald Regan masks.

Martian Food

The Martians ate my comforter and dust ruffle.
I left them alone for a minute in the bedroom
as I dashed to lay out toiletries and some towels.
Batting was everywhere. Billows of polyester
skittered like grotesque dust bunnies on the floor,
huddling around the fish tank stand and my legs.
Long green scraps draped from the table lamp
as if my bed and pillows had simply exploded.
The Martians stood there in the middle of it all.
No look of guilt. No belly bulges to belie the act done.
No sign of recognition. *This is where you sleep,*
not eat, I said. The Martian eyes were empty and flat.
I reached to grab one, and then, a second small hand.
They backed away as if I had done something wrong.

The Vanishing

The story is much bigger than frogs...
Vance Vredenburg

The Martians fill the museum for the amphibians,
a special exhibit framed in black and white,
weighted down by wooden clamps and screws.

Here, skin flames yellow and poisonous blue.
Even the stripes and spots common to yards
and state parks portends a pale underbelly.

I join the Martians to whisper, reminiscing
of creek stomping with a mason jar full
of sticks and leaves, leopard frogs, newts,

tree frogs, and toads. I explain that weeks later
my sister and I gathered tiny florescent coffins
previously full of sweet tart human bones

for the service and burial on the weedy hill
above the city river. I say, *Sometimes they died.*

Planet of the _____

*Your bones, skin hair, eyes, all the other parts of your body are
encoded in your DNA. So are all the parts of a chimpanzee's body.*
Morrill Hall Museum, Lincoln, Nebraska

The Martians compare their faces to chimpanzees.
They lift rectangular screens to theirs and see
their long, slim bodies topped with scraggy beards,
rounded brows, and brown sentient eyes.
They press their palms against the glass to test
their hand size to the animal's. They place a foot
on a raised platform with white footprints. Same
number of hairs, 99% same DNA, same fingers
same toes, human's closest relative—all noted
in the museum's learning zone display.
You lack an opposable big toe, says a Martian
who swings green legs while perching on a stool.
Everywhere the Martians explore evolution.
Masked and reflected, I can't help but to stare.

Enemy Mine

Though the film isn't set on Mars, the Martians shake.
They ask, why the humans shoot missiles at enemy ships,

why the explosion of a vessel promotes cheers, why
the only woman of color in the whole movie incinerates

within the first five minutes. They quiver at death scenes,
at crash landings, and at the pistol, knife, and laser gun.

They *ooh* and *ahh* at the crescent moons, the meteor showers,
and the landscape of red. They nod to one another, pointing, *Home*.

Eye for an Eye

The sculpture of a head on the stairs
creeps out the Martians. They can't tell

the gender. One whispers the slashes
at crown and throat suggest maleness.

The furrowed brow, the x-ed out eyes,
the lack of body makes them worry.

They ask, *What crime is punishable by head-loss?*
Where's the axe? The hooded man in black?

They're sure the body will reveal something—
wrists bound by rope or a tongue sliced out

to be set aside and buried elsewhere.
One knocks on the head. The art peals—

an empty hollow sound, a void of dead air.
Maybe, one Martian says, *it was bad thoughts.*

Last Thing You Said

Why don't you answer your damn phone?
The Martians giggle each time I replay it,
his words saved years into the future.

They like that they weren't here yet,
that earth was buried in snow, that a man
swung a hoe at his roof from the top rung

of an ladder wedged in a drift, that
why don't you sounds like an invitation,
a suggestion to help me help myself

to the possibility of interspace travel,
to meteor showers up close on my birthday,
to solar eclipses from a deck on the moon.

Answer! they chorus. *Answer!* As if I didn't
flip the phone open to the number. As if
the phone didn't shake in my hand. *Answer!*

I couldn't, but the Martians like to pretend.
They dress up in boots, hats, and scarves.
They climb the furniture and call up false gods

to stop the ice dams, open the roads,
and end the storm. They are small, angry men
and they're damned, damned if they'll take it.

Posturing

*A person who fails to recognize his or her own aggressive Martian
instincts may become the victim of violence.*
Nick Campion

The Martians worship women boxers, their fists
wrapped in gauze, their elbows cocked,
their eyes darkened with charcoal and fury.
Their braids fly like wasps around their jaw
while the Martians clutch white paper bets
and shout, *Kill 'er! Kill 'er!* for the hopeful
because everyone wishing for a good fight
sees themselves up there, feet fast on the mat,
as the striped-backed announcer backs out
of the ring and ropes, humble and small.
The Martians would bring anti-gravity shoes,
laser guns, light sabers, and poison tipped blades.
Even with these otherworldly weapons,
the Martians only ever need to use their hands.

Shrink

In the therapist's office I say, *I'm the problem,*
how I cringe while the Martians whack
the spoon against the pan of alfredo sauce,

how I snarl, *What?* whenever the Martians
talk around wads of half-chewed cheese curds
or as they slurp from mugs of hot chocolate,

how I shove the chair from the kitchen table
as the Martians slouch back and belch
in that Martian way of theirs I can't stand.

I don't like to eat, I say as I shred a tissue.
How can all those stars be so uber-tiny?
The therapist says, *The Martians are thin.*

I cry, *I know,* thinking of their green skin,
their narrow hips, their flat abdomen,
their stick-like arms and twig-like necks.

I wish I was a Martian, I sob into my hands,
imagining myself weightless, afloat in space.

Historical Study

I can't stop the Martians from their climb onto the dwarf mammoth
—15,000-years-old, three-feet-tall, and Sicilian. The skeletal cast bucks.

One Martian scales the imperial mammoth by knee, thigh, up and up
until the Martian lodges a foot into the hole of the pelvis and scrambles

onto the tail. Another grabs the hard flares of shoulder, clutches a rib,
puts a toe on the sternum, and clambers into the big bone cage. *Look!*

I've been eaten by a Mammoth. The Martian on the tail ascends higher
along the back to slide down the skull's slope to the tusk. *Watch this!*

The Martian swings back and forth to release into the air in a triple flip.
I squat near the third Martian. *Did you ever see a mammoth, for real?*

The Martian smirks and pokes me. *How old do you think we are?*
I shrug, *As old as sandhill cranes? The Platte River? The mammoths?*

The Martian tickles my side. My skin prickles in the cool museum air.
Older, the Martian says, *When the cranes sing, we know what they are singing.*

What do Martians Want

UFO skywriting...
Jeff Hecker

game
We drink tea. The Martians spot a wild turkey
on the neighbor's roof. The turkey trumpets,
walks down the shingles, crosses the street,
and trots along the walk. The Martians leave
the door open to tail the red-chinned, black
feathered creature. When the turkey pauses,
they pause and gobble. The next morning
the Martians roast fowl all day.

worship
Before dawn, the Martians commune with
daffodils. In my driveway six Martians kneel
before the yellow throats heavy with dew.
As I ride my bike to work, block after block
I see the nodding heads, the green arms,
bodies rooted to the soil below windows,
around mailboxes, by flowerbeds. I glance
at the grey ruffles of sky and worry
of late snow. Their large heads could topple.

government
The Martians claim the capitol. Some sit
on the steps and watch the sower's thrust
into the pink sunset. Some study the falcon's
nest just below the tip. Every few days, some
scale the massive shaft of Indiana marble,

until a helicopter orders them down. I ask
a nearby Martian, *Is it the shape you admire?*
Another Martian wags a finger and laughs.
It's our symbol, and points to a black tattoo
on the small of a Martian's green back: ♂.

home

The Martian tugs at the leash of a wild turkey,
Come on little Phobos. The two disappear
to a thatch of daffodils bouncing in the wind.
A group of Martians in copper armor begin
to dance. They shake spears at the Nebraska
state building and chant, *Mars vigila!*

The Left Boob of Largeness

The Martians drive me to the health clinic,
a squat brick building amid cypress,
choke cherries, and sedum tangled

in metal baskets. The Martians wait in the car
as I sit in triage an hour, two, half the day

until finally I'm seen by a red-headed nurse
to explain about my large left boob. I say,
It keeps getting bigger. It used to be a D,

same as the right, the nurse nods and types,
but then it was a little more than a D, then a DD.
Her white lab coat stretches over her bosom

and arms as she enters more of my data
and asks about my diet, exercise, and mood.
My mood *is fine,* I say, *It's my left boob.*

I lay down on the table as she palpitates,
the left, the right, and the left one again.
The white paper whispers beneath me.

When I return to the car, the Martians pat
my hand as the hazard lights flash.
We're double parked on the right, triple on the left.

I blubber into my chest as we drive along fields
of genetically modified corn and soybean,
and between the hog farms and cattle lots.

There's an alien quiet in the small space
until I say, *I'm normal.* The engine revs.
The nurse said some boobs just continue to grow.

Darn

What groans of Men shall fill the Martian Field!
Dryden tr. Virgil's *Aeneis*

The Martians felt bad about the crop circles,
six foot deep depressions in fields of corn,
while the farm hands scratch the bald slope
of their pates, slick with sweat. They pause,
ankle deep in green leaves and broken stalk,
as if sewn from above. The news had it wrong,
about which planetary species had landed,
the warm whirl of their ship's belly quilting
the earth in swoops, curls, and symmetrical lines
like this planet was really a quilting bee
and the Martians were here with threads and needles
to gossip about the new reverend and his wife,
and swap tips on stitches, like how to
mend the heels of their striped toed socks.

Martian Lie

The Martians staged Roswell. The weather balloon
was their idea, to let go a translucent bubble of silk

in the thermals above sage, agave, and compass cacti
and watch winds shred opalescent billows of fabric.

Next, they drove an old rusted jeep through sand
and deposited metal beams carved with codes

beside sheets of frail black plastic to flap and flail
against teddy bear cactus and tumbleweed, a call

to find two bodies, pale and damp with stink.
Finally, the Martians phoned the radio stations

to babble about orbs of flames, abductions,
and a crash site with odd colored lights.

Misnomer

As I sort and scoop compost into the wheelbarrow
the Martian coughs and says, *We're not from Mars.*
I crouch on my knees and push aside brittle leaves

from the worms and refuse. I respond, *If not Mars,
where are you from?* I glance from the hollow stalks
of sunflowers and withered arms of tomato plants.

The Martian sweeps away a swath of pine needles.
In the dry silt beneath, the Martian draws a canal
in a desert of saguaros. Next the Martian sketches

bison on glacial ice and spears inside Mammoth Cave.
Third, the Martian traces a labyrinth, a ball of twine,
and Minoans writing lists in a dead language

no one has yet to translate. *You're a lost people,*
I infer, *an unknown.* The Martian adds a fourth image,
a galaxy of stars and planets and a medieval sundial.

All these people, the Martian says, *have been named by you
because you didn't know what they called themselves.*
I begin to ask about the outline of three large moons,

but the Martian grabs my hand and pulls me up
until my palm is flat against the Martian's green chest.
Shhh, the Martian says, *We've never been lost.*

Porpoising

Man is his own Martian, at war against himself.
Aldous Huxley

The Martians wear spacesuits to the beach,
bubbled helmets, metallic gloves, and tubes
that ring their torso like hardened veins.

The Martians stomp the surf. They wade in,
ankle, knee, hip deep, as black waves return
broken moonlight and the red eye of Mars.

They beckon me out beyond the breakers
where they tease the undertow, tread water,
and toe the sandbars haunted by stingrays.

I pace the slick shore edged with sea foam,
permit the crash to circle my feet and calves,
but I can't go in. My eyes won't see their moons.

Epithalamion: An Undetected Life

The Martians have decided to get married.
Bridal magazines unfold on the end tables

and curl in the humidity of the bathroom.
Every weekend they take the city bus

to the mall, to David's, and to boutiques
lined with suits, tuxes, and cummerbunds.

They price check city parks, Unitarian churches,
and grassy knolls that overlook koi ponds.

They all fill out an application to officiate
because they can't decide who gets to

wear the veil or sprinkle rose petals
and who will be allowed to kiss whom.

They decorate the backyard with tulle,
fairy lights, and rows of folding chairs.

Everyone arrives, but the Martians.

Mars Vigila

Martians don't masturbate. No
    pinch or stroke. No intoxicants
of booze spiked. No Viagra.

No eye-popping size. No static
    crackle from shirt removed. No
cry to drift through open window.

No electric glow of clock light
    to illuminate small green hands
at work. Martians are not bound

by purity law. No mandatory
    ingestion of mild food. No bodies
pinned by belts and straps to stop

slow touch. No. Martians don't
    release, let go. They yearn
for Mars, their god of war.

Abduction Dream

It is the Martians with black, child-like eyes
landing a spaceship in my driveway

who will save me. Long, slim limbs,
nodding heads, wordless and listening,

the way the hands tug me from the bedclothes.
I feel only the cool of smooth skin—

flawless and scented, part apple-orchard,
part ozone. Yes: there's radiation

in outer-space, but bless these Martians
who strap me in, the Midwestern winter

gone at a push of a button, the wormholes
we propel through, the flicker of lights,

the Martians' soft gaze over the operating table
as everything inside me is opened up and touched.

The Martian Lamp

Metallic and fluted, like the body
of a man who has lifted the weight

of rock and bent iron at the command
of some master, and dusty with the grime

that collects in any home where oil burns
and the accumulation from incense and dirt

muffle all surfaces in a grey shroud,
the broad chest of the lamp beckons

the unsuspecting hand to rub and polish,
to fill the well, to light the wick, to let

the flame head grow from darkness,
offering that black tongue of smoke.

You return the lamp to the shelf, smarter now
that you've read the dial, and the word, *Aladdin,*

and remembered our imprecise language, wishes
that can turn against those you love.

Making Up

I'm not really spacey about it, I'm very here and now, but it helps me understand the Martian nature in me that wants to fight.

So we decided to stop fighting.
I agreed to turn down the volume
of my voice and open up the windows

again to allow the outdoor world
to fill our insides. The Martians
returned all the laser guns to the drawer,

put the anti-gravity boots in the closet,
and closed the lid on the tool box
of instruments for outer-space.

The Martians went out the back door
and took a long walk around the block
with the dog. I locked the front door

behind me and drove to the store
for dark chocolate and imported beer.
We got back at about the same time.

I said, *How was your day?* and kissed
the tip of each green finger. Kissing me
back, they whispered in my ear,
It just got better. How was yours?

III

...it has been remarked, we are all transplanted Martians.

Laurence Bergreen, 2000

III

American Galactic

I reach for the mailbox by shovel,
carve out a soft soliloquy.
Gauze plumes push from my lips.

I print a path from driveway
to garden to touch muted icicles
and the glass, lulled heads of mums.

Winter reveals the little sounds—
the telephone poles, gutters,
and fence posts cupped in ice,

the muffled tines of trees,
squirrels with muzzled tongues,
finches and sparrows tucked in close,

the city streets hush in snow.
Stilled behind deep, wide curtains,
the whole galaxy is home.

Deciding to Build the Spaceship

How natural if normal Martians think we produce our rocket ship
with our minds.
Ray Bradbury

The Martians gave us specs for outer-space design.
From the shopping list I had trouble with krypton,
but the Martians had some extra, so it was okay.

Once I got it all in my backyard, they took over.
The Martians spread tarp and constructed a hanger
rigged with solar panels to keep electricity bills down.

They worked for hours with tools that sparked.
Inside the flying saucer I pressed green carpet
into tack strips and washed the portholes.

When I loaded in thirteen economy-sized boxes
of astronaut food from the science center,
the Martians chuckled. Three weeks later,

the Martians sat me down under a mural
of our orbit of stars. I said, *Please, take me*
with you. The Martians shook their heads.

Green Thumbs

When Poison Ivy appears at my backyard gate
the Martians offer bouquets of Virginia creeper
and woven crowns of red-tongued honeysuckle.
I'm so startled that Dr. Isley is in my garden—

butterfly bush, tea roses, mums, and a cold frame
of lettuce, arugula, and cilantro—I gape
at her red curls glinting with evening light
and the ivy twining up and down her arms.

The Martians ignore me, gathering bouquets
of Black-eyed Susan, bee balm, and purple phlox.
In what must be a plume of pheromones, I relax
and offer her an adirondack chair. *I'm here,*

she says, *to reveal to you your secret power:*
you're a gardener. I raise an eyebrow, waving
a glove toward the lilies, herbs, and tomatoes.
I say, *I put it in the ground and see what happens.*

She presses her face into an armful of pansies,
breathes in, and then reaches for the Martians
around her. They hold her outstretched hands.
These Martins aren't beings, she says, *They're seeds.*

The moment she says this, the Martians vanish—
POP—in a flash of light. I blink in the ozone smell,

and search the yard, but all of them—Poison Ivy,
the Martians—they are entirely gone.

Lost Martians

I looked behind the dryer
where socks, mittens, and dust bunnies
crouch in shadows and lint.
I looked inside the closets.
I looked under the bed
where I've found mp3 players,
earplugs, and bad dreams.
I took a ladder outside
and looked into the treetops,
nests, and my neighbor's chimney.
I looked in bottles of screws,
dried paint cans, anti-freeze.
I looked in the mailbox.
I looked under car seats.
I looked between the towels
and the sci-fi books.
I looked inside the fridge.
I looked from the windows.
I looked through a telescope
at Mars and thought, *No*—
dry red planet, radiation,
too cold for life, *not there.*

Martian Fantasy

Sasquatch did not crash land in Roswell, New Mexico.
Sherman Alexie

I keep my mouth full of Martians, small and large ones. Around them my tongue curls and flips. I force them out in spit. I swallow Martians. Martians lodge themselves in my throat along my tonsils. Sometimes I stare deep into my esophagus and see Martians embedded in the roof or clinging to the epiglottis. Inside the crevices of my teeth are more Martians. Now and then, I want to put someone's eye out with a Martian or hurtle a Martian through a pane of glass. I build walls with Martian rock. I build bridges. I build ships. I fashion myself a tower to live in. It overlooks Martian canals. Today I want to give Martians to others, to hold them between our hands and feel the thrum. According to science, Martians are not alive and yet they're not, not alive. A Martian is forever. Under any force, Martians can't disappear entirely. It is true some Martians change person-to-person and over time they weather. If we close our eyes, could we open up to the Martians inside?

Hands like Drowned Stars: Martian Dream

The old canals filled with emptiness and dreams.
Ray Bradbury

I just had a terrible thought...what if this is a dream?
Arnold Schwarzenegger in *Total Recall*

I. *bellicose*

You boat on a brown river. You ride with the current.
The river lands sway with prairie grass and lime trees.
Low hills rise like lumps of flesh. The sun is thin gold.
The air is wet. Nothing in the world matters but this:
neither the water nor the boat's speed offers a breeze.
All motion provides the same sensation: heat and birds
moving too slow. A red hat slides by the boat. It sits
primly on the water like an iceberg. The water roils.
You pass drains like those in manmade campus ponds.
Swans bob over whatever the student body managed
to conquer: the goal post, three dozen bra and panty sets,
a bottle of scotch, a handgun, a cell phone that rings.

II. *March*

You hear it ringing, but cannot reach it, though you try.
You stick your arm all the way to the hilt. Press your face
into the surface. It rings and rings. You fondle what could
be a set of stairs, several packets of seeds, a rake, and a hoe.
Opening up your eyes underwater all you see is gold. You rise,
wipe your face on a red hat and your hands on another.
You listen. The drains make sucking noises and are rimmed
in small hairs.

III. *strange*

You ride mid-river. Strings are tied to metal loops on the boat.
Pelicans rise and fall with wing beats. The driver of the boat,
in the front rather than the back, pushes a long pole down
and lifts it up. Puffing on a slim cigarette that emits blue smoke,
the driver wears a green padded vest with hair flapping in the air.
The smoke spins from the driver's. The strings shiver. Why
does the driver feel the breeze, but not you? You lick your finger
and thrust it into the air to catch the winds, but the spit cools
on your skin. One bubble of saliva slides along your knuckle.
You rub your finger into the hat and watch the lime trees sway.

IV. *grotesque*

May I ask, you start, cough, begin again, *May I ask where
we're going?* but there is no answer. You study the hills
you pass in the boat. Some emit columns of blue smoke.
Bright orange inner tubes with fat boys in trunks pass.
They lull their tongues at you, but you can't see their eyes
because of the mirrored sunglasses. You reach to splash
them, but vertigo and a lurch in your bowels stops you.
With two hands on the boat's rim, you look over the edge.
A green hand skims the water's surface. There are ten, then
more than ten. Hands wave like stars under the surface.
You blink and blink again and yet the hands rush by you
like scotch bottles and goal posts heaved overboard.
The boys snigger. You look at your own hands ashamed.

V. *masculine*

The boat enters choppier water in a series of cannels
under the city. The boys splash and make sucking sounds.
As they float away, their echoes remain. Along the canal's
cement walkways you see bra and panty sets wadded up
like trophies. Sometimes you can see homeless men
in straw hats waiting under bridges with tomato cages.
Sometimes you pass by swans stuck in mud or dead fish
with great bloated scales and creamy, blind eyes.
They wag dead tails from the silt. *Excuse me,* you say
to the driver. *Hello? Where are we going?* No response.
You realize with a start the driver is not just a driver,
but a Martian, not one of your Martians, but one that
could've been. This Martian has wiry, sailor-like arms,
one eye, and a vest with bulging pockets—gardening gloves,
a spade, and what looks like the hard round nub of a pistol.
You wonder about a peg leg, a gold hoop through an ear,
about scurvy and syphilis coiling into the heart.

VI. *combative*

You reach into your jeans pockets and find two limes.
You place one on the hard wooden bench between you.
Take this, you say. *You don't want shingles.* Still nothing.
The other you bite into like an apple. The tang slides down
your chin and burns the back of your throat. You cough
and spit golden seeds into the water. The driver will not
acknowledge you or the lime, though the lime rolls
forward. You chew on the hard rind. It has remained
in your pockets for weeks. The second lime rolls back
to you and you kick it. It bounces against the driver's
waterproof clog. It rolls into a hole in the boat's bottom
and disappears. You put the red hat on and wish
for mirrored sunglasses, ones where no one could see you cry.

VII. *eccentric*

When the lime is gone, you lick your fingers and lean
against the boat's rear plank. It gyrates and lurches,
but you absorb the motion, hold it inside you. You try to
sing. You joke. You point out another red hat in the water.
You talk about your childhood, your mother, being made
to stand in the corner with a pelican, your life with Martians.
Opening your hands, you invite the driver to embrace you.
But nothing makes this driver Martian turn. The Martian smokes.
The vest flaps in the air. When the river calms, the Martian strips
from the vest and walks into the water, stepping into it
as if a set of stairs were there below the scrim of water.
You see no stairs from where you grip the rim. You watch
the Martian descend seven inches at a time. The last thing
to go is a thin plume of smoke.

VII. *war*

Out in the light, the city behind you, you watch pelicans.
The floating boys return, tongues wagging like fat worms.
One waves a string at you. The string is tied in a bow
on his finger. Wetness slides down his cheeks and chin
from the sunglasses. You put on a green padded vest.
It fits perfectly, snug in the right places, loose in the bad ones.
There are guns in the pockets, at least six, and a rain gauge.
You pass another red hat in the water, a swaying bank
of prairie grass and lime trees. You climb to the front
of the boat and light a cigarette that emits blue smoke.
You push a pole into the water and pull it out again.
Breeze stirs you. You don't dare study the sucking drains
or the green hands that wave at you like drowned stars.
Excuse me, someone says. *May I ask where we're going?*
A cough. *Hello?* You smoke. The breeze stirs you,
but there is nothing in this world that could make you turn
and see who sits behind you in the boat.

Close Encounters of the Third Kind

They weren't here for me,
those big-eyed creatures
who descended metal steps,
limbs long, green, and agile,
a fleet of ships behind them.

But I wanted to join them
to hold cool hands, to bend
my head toward theirs and find myself
among their ranks, shoulder
to graceful shoulder, like belonging
to an army of small gods. That kind of acceptance—
otherworldly, and stranger still—is terrifying.

You'd have to have it immediately,
be born between spindly legs into a red
territory so windswept and dry
that you would always thirst and suckle
from something more intelligent than you.
In that cradle, you would play with lunar
gardening, mind control, and infinite, cold space.

They didn't want me.
Still, when they came that night
with lights and sound that shook
the darkness around us, we all glowed
for one brief cinematic moment,
I believed they did.

Notes

The opening and section epigraphs are from the following: *The World Doesn't End* (Harcourt Brace & Company, 1985) by Charles Simic (63); *Voyage to Mars: NASA's Search for Life Beyond Earth* (Riverhead Books, 2000) by Laurence Bergreen (204); *Something Wicked This Way Comes* (Simon & Schuster, 1962) by Ray Bradbury; and *War of the Worlds* (William Heinemann, 1898) by H. G. Wells (210).

"Between Lands": as quoted in *Strangers in the Night: A Brief History of Life on Other Worlds* (Counterpoint, 1998) by David E. Fisher and Marshall Jon Fisher (19).

"Warning": quotation from John Berryman's "Dreamsong 4."

"Rocket Summer": title taken the first chapter of *The Martian Chronicles* (William Morrow, 2006) by Ray Bradbury. Quotation from (5).

"Getting Out of Here": quotation from "To Boldly Go Where No Tomato Has Gone Before: Growing Plants on the Moon" by Alaina G. Levine in *Arizona Alumnus,* Vol 88.1, Fall 2010 (10-11).

"The Tabloids": quotation adapted from an article on Kenneth Arnold on Wikipedia.

"Arrival": quotation from Eleanor Lerman's "We're Ready in Roswell" in *Our Post-Soviet History Unfolds* (Sarabande Books, 2005).

"First Contact": quotation from *Parable of the Talents* (Seven Stories Press, 1998, and Recorded books, 2001) by Octavia E. Butler, disc 2.

"South of the Train Tracks": quotation from *Caitline his conspiracy* (1611) by Ben Jonson.

"A Star": quotation from *The News Chronicle* (London), 2 June 1953, 1/1.

"The Martian Order": quotation from *Four Quartets* (Mariner Books, 1968) by T. S. Elliot (59).

"Protest": quotation from "Crisis in Egypt-Anderson Cooper and Bill O'Reilly," *The Colbert Report* (video), February 3, 2011.
<http://www.colbertnation.com/the-cobert-report-videos/373357/february-03-2011/crisis-in-egypt---anderson-cooper---bill-o-reily=>

"The Vanishing": quotation from the banner that appeared in "The Vanishing" special exhibit by Joel Sarforce, Morrill Hall, Lincoln, Nebraska December 2010 – November 2011. The banner excerpted Jennifer S. Holland's piece "The Vanishing," *National Geographics Magazine*, April 2009.

"Planet of the _____": quotation from Morrill Hall's permanent exhibit on chimpanzees and their relationship to humans, 2011.

"Enemy Mine": titled after the movie with the same name.

"Eye for an Eye": responds to the bronze sculpture *Fallen Dreamer* (1995) by Tom Otterness, on display on the steps of the Sheldon Art Museum, Lincoln, Nebraska.

"Posturing": after Delilah Montonye photograph of Dorren Hilton, 2006, collected at the Sheldon Art Museum in Lincoln, Nebraska. Quotation from *The Practical Astrologer* (Hamyln, 1993) by Nick Campion.

"Historical Study": responds to the permanent mammoth exhibit in Morrill Hall.

"What do Martians Want": quotation from "def" in *Hornbook* (Horseless Press, 2012) by Jeffrey Hecker.

"Darn": after Marilyn Bridges photograph "Spiral in Field" Hennietta, N.Y. 1981, displayed at the Sheldon Art Museum, Lincoln, Nebraska in March 2011. Quotation from *The works of Virgil: containing his Pastorals, Georgics, and Æneis* (Jacob Tonson, 1697) by Virgil and translated John Dryden, 1st edition, Vol. 1.

"Porpoising": quotation from *Themes and Variations* (1950) by Aldous Huxley (239).

"Making Up": quotation from *Kindred Sprit Quarterly* (Devon, U.K.), Autumn 1994, 46/1.

"Deciding to Build the Spaceship": quotation from Bradbury.

"Martian Dream": quotation from *The Summer of Black Widows* (Hanging Loose Press, 1996) by Sherman Alexie (109).

"Hands like Drowned Stars: Martian Dream": quotation from Bradbury; second quotation from Arnold Schwarzenegger's character Douglas Quaid in the film *Total Recall.*

"Close Encounters of the Third Kind": titled after the movie with the same name.

Acknowledgements

Grateful appreciation is expressed to the editors and staff of the following publications in which these poems or versions of these poems first appeared:

A cappella Zoo: "Hands Like Drowned Stars: Martian Dream"

Apostrophe: "Getting Out of Here"

Bat Shat: "Stranger Still"

Handful of Dust: "Arrival"

The Delinquent: "Last Thing You Said," "Making Up"

Interrobang?! Magazine!: "The Tabloids," "Between Lands, Part II"

Labletter: "First Contact," "Martian Food," "Misnomer," "Why Not to Buy Martians Sundaes Topped with Cherries"

Martian Lit: "Epithalamion: An Undetected Life," "Mars Vigila," "Green Thumb," "Lost Martians"

Message in a Bottle: "Enemy Mine," "Warning," "Reality TV: The Trouble with Martians is They Don't Fit In," "After Watching a Martian Marathon on Cable," "The Martians Order"

Mixed Fruit: "The Vanishing"

Moondance: "Rocket Summer: A Memory"

New Contrast: "Close Encounters of the Third Kind," "Eye for an Eye"

Penwood Review: "What Martians Wish"

Prime Number: "What Martians Want," "Historical Study," "Porpoising"

Rose Red Review: "Creed: The Mission"

Silver Blade: "Protest," "Martian Lie," "Darn," "Planet of the _____",
   "Eye for an Eye"

Scissor Tale Review: "American Galactic"

South Florida Arts Journal: "A Star," "Shrink," "The Left Boob of Largeness,"
   "Deciding to Build the Spaceship"

Strange Horizons: "Abduction Dream"

Thirteen Myna Birds: "Posturing"

The Whistling Fire: "Martian Fantasy"

"Between Lands, Part I" first appeared in the anthology *Multi Culti Mixterations: Playful and Profound Interpretations of Culture Through Haiku*. Richard H. McNab, Ed. 2011.

"Posturing" and "Housekeeping with Martians" first appeared in a limited edition series of broadsides with artwork by Kate Johnson. Peoria, IL: Prairie Center of the Arts, 2011.

"Misnomer" was reprinted with permission in the anthology *Science Poetry*. Neil Harding McAlister and Zara McAlister, Eds. Port Perry, Ontario, Canada: McAlister, Neil Harding, 2011.

"The Martian Lamp" first appeared in a digital poetry by Adam Wagler. Peoria, IL: Prairie Center of the Arts, 2012.

"South of the Train Tracks" first appeared in the anthology *Every River on Earth: Writing from Appalachian Ohio.* Neil Carpathios, Ed. Athens, OH: Ohio University Press, 2013.

"First Contact," "Martian Food," and "Misnomer," were performed in *Bottom's Dream/Martian Tales* at the Theatre Wit in Chicago, April 30, 2013.

Several of these poems also appeared in the chapbook *Stranger Still* (Finishing Line Press, 2013).

~

This book was made possible by funds granted to the author: the Louise Van Sickle Fellowship in Creative Writing, the Louise Pound Fellowship, the Stuff Memorial Fellowship, and a Graduate Studies Fellowship from the University of Nebraska-Lincoln. I am extremely grateful for the support of the colleagues and staff at UNL. Thanks to The Helene Wurlitzer Foundation of New Mexico for the residency and grant during which this manuscript was finalized for press.

I want to thank those who planned, organized, and guided the unofficial co-ed Iowa State University spring break trip to New Mexico in 2000, including an exploration of the International UFO Museum and Research Center in Roswell. I want to thank those who've supported my study of sci-fi literature, film, and TV, especially Kay McCollen who taught the work of David Brin in AP English and gave the a graduation gift of *The Collected Poems of Emily Dickinson* with the inscription, "May your life be filled with dreams, love, joy, and poetry!" I want to especially thank the poet Naomi Shihab Nye who encouraged me to write these poems that were begun in her master workshop in poetry at UNL in 2009. I want to thank my students in composition, poetry, and creative writing who joined me in writing in-class poems and on writing field trips to the Sheldon Art Museum and University of Nebraska State Museum where several of these poems were first written.

About the Author

Laura Madeline Wiseman has a doctorate from the University of Nebraska-Lincoln where she teaches English and creative writing. She is the author of twelve collections of poetry, including the full-length book *Sprung* (San Francisco Bay Press, 2012) the letterpress books *Unclose the Door* (Gold Quoin Press, 2012) and *Farm Hands* (Gold Quoin Press, 2012), and the chapbooks *First Wife* (Hyacinth Girl Press, 2013), *Stranger Still* (Finishing Line Press, 2013), *Men and Their Whims* (Writing Knights Press, 2013), *She Who Loves Her Father* (Dancing Girl Press, 2012), *Branding Girls* (Finishing Line Press, 2011), *Ghost Girl* (Pudding House Publications, 2010), and *My Imaginary* (Dancing Girl Press, 2010). She is also the editor of *Women Write Resistance: Poets Resist Gender Violence* (Hyacinth Girl Press, 2013). Her poetry, short stories, essays, and reviews have appeared in *Prairie Schooner, Margie, Arts & Letters, Poet Lore,* and *Feminist Studies.* She has received an Academy of American Poets Award, a Mari Sandoz/Prairie Schooner Award, a Susan Atefact Peckham Fellowship, a Louise Van Sickle Fellowship, and grants from the Kimmel Harding Nelson Center for the Arts, the Center for the Great Plains Studies, and the Wurlitzer Foundation of New Mexico. www.lauramadelinewiseman.com

Other Books by Laura Madeline Wiseman

BOOKS

Intimates and Fools (Les Femme Folles Books, 2014) with artist Sally Deskins

Queen of the Platform (Anaphora Literary Press, 2013)

Women Write Resistance: Poets Resist Gender Violence, editor (Hyacinth Girl Press, 2013)

Sprung (San Francisco Bay Press, 2012)

LETTERPRESS BOOKS

Unclose the Door (Gold Quoin Press, 2012)

Farm Hands (Gold Quoin Press, 2012)

CHAPBOOKS

Stranger Still (Finishing Line Press, 2013)

First Wife (Hyacinth Girl Press, 2013)

Men and Their Whims (Writing Knights Press, 2013)

She Who Loves Her Father (Dancing Girl Press, 2012)

Branding Girls (Finishing Line Press, 2011)

Ghost Girl (Pudding House Publications, 2010)

My Imaginary (Dancing Girl Press, 2010)

www.ingramcontent.com/pod-product-compliance
Lightning Source LLC
Chambersburg PA
CBHW070614060426
42445CB00038B/1171